Original title:
Joyful Wings in Flight

Author: Aron Pilviste
ISBN HARDBACK: 978-9908-1-4435-1
ISBN PAPERBACK: 978-9908-1-4436-8
ISBN EBOOK: 978-9908-1-4437-5

Boundless Euphoria of the Sky

Beneath the sky so vast and wide,
Clouds like dreams begin to glide.
Sunlight dances, warm and bright,
In this space, we find our flight.

Soft whispers of the evening breeze,
Waves of peace among the trees.
Stars awaken, one by one,
A tapestry of night begun.

Colors merge as day does fade,
Nature's art in light displayed.
Horizon sings with hues so rare,
In this beauty, we find our prayer.

Moments linger, time stands still,
Every heartbeat, every thrill.
Boundless joy in every sigh,
Here beneath the endless sky.

In this realm, our spirits soar,
Dancing freely evermore.
Embraced by night, kissed by day,
Boundless euphoria leads the way.

Gossamer Threads of Joy

Delicate whispers in the air,
Twinkling stars beyond compare.
Moments woven through each day,
Joyful hearts in soft ballet.

Feel the warmth of friendship's light,
Gentle smiles that feel so bright.
Gossamer threads, we hold them tight,
Painting dreams in pure delight.

Journey Beyond the Rainbow

Beneath the arch where colors blend,
Wanderers seek, their dreams to send.
Paths of gold in skies above,
Guided by the stars they love.

With each step, new wonders found,
Magic whispers all around.
Fortune smiles on those who dare,
In the journey, joys to share.

Laughter in the Wind

Echoing through the trees so high,
Laughter dances, a sweet sigh.
Carefree moments in gentle breeze,
Lift the spirits, hearts at ease.

Every giggle, a spark of light,
Filling shadows with pure delight.
Nature's song, a merry blend,
A symphony that will not end.

A Flight of Fancy

Dreams take wing on feathered flight,
Through the clouds, beyond the night.
Imagination paints the sky,
On whispered winds, we drift and fly.

Daring souls who seek the stars,
Chasing shadows, forgetting scars.
In our hearts, a freedom grand,
Together in this wonderland.

Colors on the Horizon

The sun begins to rise,
Casting shades of gold,
Blues blend with oranges,
A canvas to behold.

As the day awakens,
All colors intertwine,
A dance of light and warmth,
In nature's grand design.

Pink whispers touch the skies,
While purple shadows play,
Each hue tells a story,
Of a brand new day.

Clouds drift in soft silence,
Painted in pastels bright,
A symphony of colors,
At dawn's gentle light.

The horizon stretches wide,
With wonders to explore,
Each moment glowing rare,
Inviting us for more.

The Art of Rising High

In the morning's embrace,
Dreams begin to soar,
With wings wide open,
We strive to explore.

Mountains stand before us,
Tall and proud they gleam,
With every step we take,
We strengthen our dream.

Clouds float like the whispers,
Of hopes we can't contain,
The art of rising high,
Is dancing through the rain.

With each challenge faced,
We climb to reach the sky,
In the heart of struggle,
True strength will never die.

So let the spirit rise,
Through valleys and the mist,
With courage as our guide,
Embrace what we have wished.

Embrace the Gentle Breeze

A whisper through the trees,
Nature's softest sigh,
The breeze carries secrets,
As it dances by.

With every gentle touch,
It wraps us in its grace,
A tender reminder,
Of a warm embrace.

Leaves sway in delight,
As laughter fills the air,
The gentle breeze inspires,
A moment to share.

Close your eyes and feel,
The freedom all around,
In the arms of nature,
Our souls can be unbound.

So take a breath of peace,
Let troubles drift away,
Embrace the gentle breeze,
In the light of day.

Heartbeats Among the Clouds

Above the world we rise,
Where dreams learn to take flight,
Heartbeats mix with whispers,
In the calm of night.

Stars twinkle in the dark,
Guiding us with their light,
Floating on our wishes,
As we drift in height.

Clouds cradle our thoughts,
Soft as a lover's sigh,
A sanctuary found,
Where stars and dreams lie.

Feel the pulse of the sky,
As we chase the unknown,
In the arms of the heavens,
We find a place called home.

Together, hand in hand,
We'll write our story's prose,
With heartbeats among clouds,
As our journey unfolds.

Skies Awash with Delight

In the blush of dawn's first light,
Clouds drift softly, pure and white.
Colors mingle, bright and bold,
Stories of new days unfold.

Harbors of hope in sunlit hue,
Winds whisper secrets, old yet new.
Nature sings in cheerful chords,
Harmony flows, our hearts aboard.

Fields adorned with flowers bright,
Dancing petals in perfect flight.
Sunbeams kiss the morning dew,
Each moment feels like a dream come true.

Mountains high, where eagles soar,
Embracing heights, forevermore.
Every shadow, every ray,
Guides our souls to joy’s ballet.

As dusk descends, the stars ignite,
Each twinkle holds a wish in sight.
Skies awash with pure delight,
Embrace the magic of the night.

Echoes of Effervescent Joy

Laughter bubbles, bright and clear,
Joy cascades, we draw it near.
A melody that lifts us high,
In every heart, a buoyant sky.

Chasing dreams on vibrant streams,
In every step, the sunlight gleams.
Together we weave tales so grand,
In the warmth of kinship's hand.

Ripples dance on tranquil lakes,
Embracing moments, the joy that wakes.
Happiness in every glance,
In this life, we find our dance.

With every hug, compassion spreads,
Inspiring smiles, as kindness spreads.
Whispers of hope on gentle winds,
In this life, true joy rescinds.

Echoes linger, soft and bright,
In our hearts, purest delight.
A tapestry of laughter sewn,
In the space we call our own.

Horizon’s Laughter

Beyond the hills, where colors gleam,
Hope arises, like a dream.
Sunset paints the sky with fire,
Awakens in us, deep desire.

Whispers travel on the breeze,
Carried forth with perfect ease.
A symphony of twilight song,
In nature's arms, we all belong.

The day retreats, the stars appear,
Offering beauty, calm and clear.
Each twinkle holds a tale untold,
A dance of secrets, bright and bold.

Together we watch as shadows play,
Golden horizons greet the day.
In every heartbeat, laughter flows,
In every moment, love still grows.

Dancing dreams on the horizon’s edge,
Life unfolds like a sacred pledge.
Through every turn, we find our way,
In the laughter of the day.

The Dance of Life’s Feathered Inspirations

In the morning light so fair,
Birds take flight through fragrant air.
Wings unfurl in gentle grace,
In the sky, they find their place.

From blossoms sweet, they draw their song,
Nature’s choir, where we belong.
Each note a whisper, soft and true,
They dance through clouds—the sky so blue.

The rustle of leaves, a tender sigh,
In the rhythm of life, we learn to fly.
With every flap, a story's spun,
In harmony, we all are one.

Through every season, they inspire,
Filling our hearts with sweet desire.
A ballet played on currents’ rise,
Life's dance unfolds beneath the skies.

Embrace the beauty, let it flow,
Let your spirit take its glow.
In every heartbeat, feel the call,
For life’s dance beckons one and all.

Ascending Smiles

In a garden of dreams, they bloom,
Bright laughter spills, dispelling gloom.
Each smile a star, lighting the night,
A gentle warmth, pure and bright.

With every whisper, joy takes flight,
In the chorus of hearts, pure delight.
A dance of souls, hand in hand,
Together we rise, together we stand.

The sun kisses cheeks, glowing wide,
In this moment, there's nothing to hide.
Each heartbeat echoes, strong and true,
In the sea of smiles, we renew.

Through valleys deep and mountains high,
Our laughter echoes, reaching the sky.
With every step, we weave a tale,
Of joy and love that will not pale.

As dawn breaks forth, the world awake,
With every smile, new chances we make.
In this journey, hand in hand we roam,
Together in joy, we find our home.

Skyward Bound Harmony

Underneath the endless blue,
We chase the dreams that feel so true.
With wings of hope, we rise and fly,
In harmony, we touch the sky.

Each note we sing, a gentle breeze,
Whispers of love in rustling trees.
Notes intertwine, so soft and sweet,
In this symphony, our hearts meet.

As clouds drift by, in silver hue,
Our spirits soar, painting the view.
Together we dance on a canvas wide,
In every heartbeat, there's beauty inside.

The sun dips low, a golden glow,
In twilight's embrace, our joy will flow.
With every flicker, stars appear,
A melody of hope, crystal clear.

With laughter echoing, hearts in tune,
We weave our dreams beneath the moon.
In this boundless sky, love knows no end,
In every note, we rise, transcend.

Echoing Bliss

In whispers soft, the joy we share,
Resonates, like a sweet prayer.
Each heartbeat sings, a gentle groove,
In this moment, we rise and move.

Through valleys deep, our laughter runs,
Shining bright like the morning sun.
With every step, our spirits twine,
In this dance of love, we will shine.

Feel the rhythm, the world awake,
In every echo, bonds we make.
Joy travels far, like ripples spread,
Together in bliss, where hearts are led.

The nightingale calls, a song so sweet,
In every melody, our souls meet.
With open arms, we embrace the light,
In the echo of bliss, we take flight.

So let us wander, hand in hand,
In this echo, we understand.
Together we write our joyful quest,
In the melody of life, we find rest.

Wings That Paint the Sky

With painted wings, we soar so high,
Across the canvas of the sky.
In hues of hope, we spread our dreams,
In every color, the heart redeems.

As sunlight dances on feathered grace,
We chase horizons, time can't erase.
In freedom's embrace, our spirits glide,
In this flight of joy, we take pride.

The stars align in a cosmic show,
As we ride the winds, calm and slow.
In every sunset's warm embrace,
We find our place, our sacred space.

Beneath the moon, our laughter sways,
With every heartbeat, love displays.
In the vast expanse, we are one,
Together we rise, a journey begun.

Through clouds of dreams, we paint the night,
In every heartbeat, we find our light.
With wings of love, forever we fly,
In the tapestry of life, you and I.

The Radiant Escape

In golden rays, we find our way,
Where shadows dance and colors play.
With hearts ablaze, we soar so high,
Embracing freedom, we touch the sky.

The world awaits, a canvas bright,
Adventure calls with pure delight.
Together we chase the morning light,
In joyful whispers, dreams take flight.

From hills to valleys, laughter rings,
A symphony of life unfolds and sings.
With every step, new wonders gleam,
In this radiant escape, we dream.

Through forests deep, and rivers wide,
We'll navigate with hearts as our guide.
Each moment shared, a treasure found,
In this embrace, we stand unbound.

As twilight falls, the stars appear,
With every glance, we conquer fear.
In the distance, home awaits us near,
In love's warm glow, we persevere.

Wings of Unfolding Laughter

With laughter bright as morning sun,
We spread our wings, our hearts are one.
In playful skies, our spirits rise,
A dance of joy in endless skies.

The world transforms with every sound,
In giggles soft, pure bliss we've found.
We drift on dreams, like whispers light,
In laughter's embrace, we take our flight.

Through fields of flowers, we'll wander free,
Painting the air with harmony.
Each moment shared, sweet melodies,
In nature's grace, we find our ease.

With friends beside, the journey's clear,
In joyful hearts, we conquer fear.
Together we'll chase the fleeting day,
With wings of laughter, we'll find our way.

As dusk descends, our spirits shine,
In every smile, love intertwines.
We'll carry forth this light, so bright,
With wings of joy, we claim the night.

Spirit's Ascent

In the stillness of a whispered prayer,
The spirit rises, free as air.
With every breath, we journey on,
Into the light, till darkness gone.

Each soul a star, unique and bright,
Illuminating the endless night.
Together we climb, hand in hand,
In unity, we make our stand.

Through trials faced, we learn and grow,
In every heart, our courage shows.
With faith as wings, we break the chains,
In the spirit's ascent, freedom reigns.

In the echo of the ancient past,
We find the strength to hold steadfast.
The winds of change may challenge us,
But in our hearts, we place our trust.

As we soar high, the clouds we'll taste,
In every moment, love embraced.
Our spirits dance, like flames aglow,
In the ascent, we'll always grow.

A Ballet in the Breeze

Beneath the trees, where soft winds play,
A ballet blooms at close of day.
With graceful moves, the leaves entwine,
A dance of nature, so divine.

As petals twirl in sweet repose,
In this soft hush, the magic flows.
With every gust, a story spins,
In whispers shared, the beauty wins.

Through fields adorned in colors bright,
The world becomes a canvas light.
With every breath, a dance we weave,
In nature's arms, we truly believe.

With twilight's touch, the stars premiere,
A symphony that draws us near.
We sway with joy, in soft embrace,
In the ebb and flow, we find our place.

The moon above, a guiding light,
As dreams take flight, we are the night.
With every step, a story's spun,
In this ballet, we are one.

Celestial Rhapsody

Stars dance above with bright delight,
In twilight's glow, they paint the night.
Galaxies whisper tales of old,
In cosmic dreams, their secrets unfold.

Planets sway in celestial grace,
Each orbit a silent, sacred space.
The moon sings softly, a lullaby,
Guiding lost souls through the night sky.

Nebulas bloom in vibrant hues,
Cradling stardust, a cosmic muse.
Constellations weave a timeless thread,
Binding the universe, where dreams are fed.

Comets streak in fleeting blaze,
Lighting pathways through the haze.
In this vastness, we find our place,
Within the rhapsody of cosmic embrace.

With every twinkle, hope takes flight,
In the celestial dance, we find our light.
Together we roam this endless sea,
In the rhapsody where we’re always free.

The Happiness of Unbroken Flight

Wings spread wide against the blue,
Above the clouds where dreams come true.
A world below, so small and bright,
In freedom's arms, we take our flight.

Feathers brush the whispering air,
In every glide, we shed our care.
With every beat, our spirits soar,
Chasing horizons, forevermore.

The sun kisses our daring hearts,
In this vast sky, adventure starts.
Through storms and calm, we boldly glide,
In the joy, the winds can't hide.

Nature's breeze guides our questing souls,
In this ballet, our spirit rolls.
Each moment savored, time stands still,
In unbroken flight, we find our will.

Boundless skies, our dreams alight,
In the happiness of sheer delight.
Together we dance, in perfect sight,
In the embrace of unbroken flight.

Fables in the Sky

Clouds drift slowly, tales unfold,
In their whispers, a story told.
Characters born from sun and rain,
Each fragment a memory, a joyful gain.

Dragons soar on wings of white,
Guardians of realms, in endless flight.
Castles rise high on cotton beds,
Where imagination gently treads.

Stars are scribes in the velvet night,
Writing fables in silvery light.
They weave together time and space,
In every twinkle, a fleeting trace.

Moonlit paths lead wanderers forth,
To secret places of great worth.
In the sky's embrace, dreams intertwine,
As we search for the stories divine.

Fables linger in the evening glow,
A tapestry of wonder, ebb and flow.
Here in the sky, our hearts ignite,
In the dance of dreams, we find our flight.

The Sky’s Melodic Embrace

In twilight's hush, the sky hums low,
A soothing tune, a gentle flow.
Each star a note in harmony,
Composing peace for you and me.

Clouds drift softly, a soft refrain,
Whispering secrets of joy and pain.
The sun bows down, a golden grace,
In the sky’s arms, we find our place.

Raindrops patter like soft applause,
Nature’s rhythm, without a pause.
Thunder rolls with a mighty sound,
In this embrace, our dreams are found.

In every breeze, a melody sings,
The sky’s embrace, a gift it brings.
With open hearts, we feel the beat,
In nature's symphony, life feels complete.

So lift your gaze, let your worries cease,
In the sky's embrace, discover peace.
Together we bask in the endless space,
In the sweet and timeless melodic embrace.

Blissful Ascendancy

In the dawn's gentle light, they rise,
Dreams woven in soft, bright skies.
Mountains echo with a soothing song,
In this realm, we all belong.

Hearts alight with joy and grace,
Every moment, an embrace.
Whispers dance on the morning breeze,
Filling souls with tranquil ease.

Golden rays begin to glow,
Painting worlds in a soft flow.
Hands held tight, we reach for more,
Together, we'll forever soar.

With each step, the spirit grows,
In life's garden, love bestows.
Rise above the earth's sweet call,
Embracing hope, we will not fall.

In unity, our voices blend,
Through every curve, around each bend.
Blissful hearts shall ever sing,
In this life, we find our wings.

Dancing with the Air

Whirls of laughter in a breeze,
Nature's pulse, an endless tease.
Step by step, we twirl and sway,
Kissed by light on a vibrant day.

Twilight whispers secrets near,
Filling our hearts with joy and cheer.
We become one with the sky,
In every leap, we learn to fly.

Through the fields, we shall roam,
With spirits wild, we feel at home.
The stars above, our shining guide,
With open arms, we face the tide.

Every moment we embrace,
In this dance, we find our place.
A symphony of dreams takes flight,
Together, we ignite the night.

As the sun dips low and fair,
We whisper secrets to the air.
With every turn, we paint the sky,
This is where our spirits fly.

Ethereal Journeys in Brilliance

In twilight’s embrace, we take flight,
Stars awaken, illuminating the night.
With every heartbeat, a story unfolds,
Adventures await in the tales retold.

Through wisps of clouds, we drift and dream,
Casting visions on the silver stream.
Every glimmer, a path revealed,
In our souls, the magic's sealed.

The moon’s soft glow, a guiding light,
Leading us through the depths of night.
In the silence, our hearts conspire,
With each moment, we climb higher.

Voices echo in endless space,
Caught in a timeless, sweet embrace.
Journey forth, fear not the unknown,
Within us lies a love that’s grown.

As dawn breaks with its golden hue,
Each step anew, our dreams accrue.
Together we weave a dance divine,
In ethereal realms, our spirits shine.

The Exuberance of Endless Skies

Above the clouds, we find our grace,
In endless skies, we embrace.
Heartbeats echo, wild and free,
Wings of joy carry us to be.

Fleeting moments, a vibrant hue,
The world awakens, fresh and new.
With every sunrise, dreams take flight,
In azure depths, we find our light.

Chaos fades, tranquility reigns,
In whispered winds, love remains.
From valleys low to mountains high,
Together we soar, you and I.

The horizon beckons, bright and clear,
Every journey, a tale to cheer.
In every heartbeat, life unfolds,
Exuberant stories waiting to be told.

Across the vastness, we wander bold,
In the tapestry of life we hold.
Guided by stars, our spirits ascend,
In the embrace of skies, we transcend.

The Exhilaration of Altitude

Atop the world, I stand so free,
With whispers of the sky calling me.
Each breath a thrill, each glance a prize,
Beneath the vast and endless skies.

Clouds like pillows, soft and bright,
Embrace my spirit, take my flight.
The sun is warming, my heart it fills,
As pure joy dances on the hills.

Stars above, a twinkling show,
Guide me gently where dreams can grow.
The thrill of heights, a sweet delight,
In this vast realm of pure, pure light.

Eagles soar in circles wide,
With wind beneath, I take my stride.
Freedom sings in every cheer,
The altitude brings visions clear.

And in this space, I find my heart,
A sense of peace, a brand new start.
The world below, a distant hum,
In the exhilaration, I become.

Ascension of the Happy Soul

Rise up high, where dreams take flight,
A joyful spirit, a heart so light.
The clouds invite, the sun does shine,
In this ascent, my soul aligns.

With every step, I shed my fear,
The heights I reach, a vision clear.
Each smile shared in skies so blue,
An ascension blessed, forever true.

The whispering winds sing songs of old,
Of happy souls and hearts bold.
The journey brightens, the view expands,
With open minds and outstretched hands.

In golden rays, I feel embraced,
By laughter echoing, joy interlaced.
The world below starts to fade,
In this high dance, my soul is made.

So let us rise with hearts aglow,
In every step, new joys to sow.
Ascension calls, let's take the leap,
In happiness, our dreams we'll keep.

The Magic of Soaring Dreams

Dreams take wings like birds in flight,
Through starry realms, they spark delight.
With every whisper, we ascend high,
On currents of hope that never die.

Magic brews in the evening glow,
As imagination begins to flow.
In the silence, we hear the call,
Of dreams that soar above us all.

Fleeting moments, catching light,
We navigate the endless night.
With hearts ablaze and spirits bright,
We chase the dreams that feel so right.

Each wish a feather, each thought a spark,
Guiding our journey through realms so dark.
The magic of dreams, a powerful thread,
Lifting us high where hopes are fed.

So let us dance in silver beams,
Embrace the magic of all our dreams.
In this vast sky, together we glide,
Boundless and free, our hearts open wide.

Airborne Laughter

In the breeze, laughter ignites,
Floating freely, it takes to heights.
Joyful echoes, crisp and clear,
In airborne realms, we shed our fear.

With every chuckle, we rise and spin,
The world's weight, we shake off, and win.
Together we soar, a jovial crew,
In the air, our happiness grew.

Clouds embrace with soft delight,
In playful spirit, we dance tonight.
A chorus of giggles we weave and share,
As laughter drifts upon the air.

Beneath the sun, we churn and glide,
On waves of mirth, we quickly ride.
Boundless joy in every sound,
In airborne laughter, peace is found.

So let us rise, let our voices soar,
With each shared laugh, we crave for more.
In this carefree flight, we find our way,
Airborne laughter brightens the day.

The Serenade of Open Skies

Beneath the azure, dreams take flight,
Whispers of clouds, soft and light.
Where the sun paints horizons bright,
In the heart of day, pure delight.

Gentle breezes hum a tune,
As flowers dance beneath the moon.
Nature's chorus, a sweet boon,
Echoing love on the afternoon.

Each star afloat in the night sea,
Guides lost wanderers to be free.
In every shadow, a memory,
Captured in time, eternally.

Above the world in a blissful trance,
We find ourselves in a cosmic dance.
With every heartbeat, a new chance,
To embrace life’s vast expanse.

So let us dream beneath this dome,
In the serenade of heart and home.
With every sigh, a wish to roam,
Among the stars, forever known.

Beneath the Feathered Canopy

In the embrace of leaves so green,
Life whispers softly in between.
With every flicker, a new scene,
Nature's wonders, pure and serene.

Birds weave tales in the morning glow,
Their melodies set the world aglow.
Through thick branches, gentle breezes flow,
Beneath the canopy, time moves slow.

Sunlight filters with a golden hue,
Painting shadows that dance anew.
Each rustle speaks of wonders true,
In this paradise, me and you.

The forest breathes a timeless sigh,
As butterflies flutter and wink goodbye.
In this haven, we learn to fly,
Under the watch of the endless sky.

So let us dwell in this sacred space,
With nature's arms, our warm embrace.
In the hush of leaves, we find our place,
Beneath the canopy, life’s true grace.

Crescendo of Blissful Echoes

In moments still, the world awakes,
Harmony flows in gentle lakes.
Whispers of joy, our spirit takes,
In the quiet, the heart remakes.

With every note, the soul ignites,
A symphony of soaring heights.
Through valleys deep, and starry nights,
Music of life, love’s purest rights.

Echoes of laughter fill the air,
In melodies crafted with care.
Each heartbeat dances without a care,
In the cadence, we find our prayer.

Resonance spreads through fields of gold,
A story of dreams quietly told.
In the rhythm, a life unfolds,
As we embrace the warmth of old.

So let us tune our souls to bliss,
In every moment, a gentle kiss.
Life's crescendo, we cannot miss,
In echoes of love, we find our bliss.

A Journey Through Aether

In the twilight, dreams take flight,
Navigating through the silent night.
Stars align, a wondrous sight,
Guiding souls with ancient light.

Through the aether, we gently soar,
Exploring realms we can't ignore.
With every heartbeat, we seek more,
In the vastness, our spirits roar.

Whispers of the cosmos call our name,
In this voyage, we’re never the same.
Fuelled by wonder, passion, and flame,
Through time and space, we stake our claim.

In every galaxy, a tale unfolds,
With mysteries that the heart beholds.
Together we weave where stardust molds,
In this journey, our spirit holds.

So let us wander, hand in hand,
Through the aether, across this land.
In the boundless skies, we understand,
We are forever, endless and grand.

Chasing Radiance Above the Clouds

In the dawn, colors bloom bright,
Whispers of gold in morning light.
We chase the glow, hearts set free,
Dancing in dreams, just you and me.

Floating high where eagles soar,
The world below, an open door.
In silence, we find our sound,
As joy and laughter swirl around.

On a canvas of sky, we write,
Our hopes and wishes take to flight.
With every breath, the breeze will sing,
Of all the wonder that love can bring.

Through the haze, the sun will peek,
A tender touch, the light we seek.
In this moment, we'll forever stay,
Chasing radiance, come what may.

Above the clouds, the view so grand,
Hand in hand, we make our stand.
With faith and dreams, we'll break the mold,
In a world where hearts are bold.

Gleeful Horizons Unfold

With laughter bright, the world awakes,
Soft whispers of joy, the morning takes.
Gleeful horizons stretch ahead,
In golden rays, our spirits wed.

Through fields of green, we run and play,
Chasing the shadows of yesterday.
With every step, new paths we find,
In the dance of joy, our hearts entwined.

The sun dips low, painted skies,
Reflections of dreams in each sunrise.
We hold our breath as colors blend,
In this beautiful journey, we transcend.

With every heartbeat, life unfolds,
In tales of love, our future molds.
Together we dream, together we shine,
In the tapestry of life, you're forever mine.

As stars ignite the evening's grace,
In the stillness, we find our place.
Hand in hand, with spirits bold,
We embrace the beauty as stories unfold.

A Symphony of Soaring Hearts

In the whispering wind, our dreams take flight,
Melodies dance in the soft twilight.
A symphony plays, hearts intertwine,
In the rhythm of love, you are mine.

With each crescendo, the world anew,
Notes of laughter echo, pure and true.
Together we sway in the moonlight’s glow,
In a harmony only we can know.

Through valleys deep, and mountains high,
Chasing the stars that light the sky.
In every heartbeat, a sound so sweet,
In this concert of life, our souls meet.

As the dawn breaks, a new refrain,
Promises whispered, joy and pain.
A tapestry woven with every part,
Our symphony sings of soaring hearts.

In the quiet moments, our love will play,
A timeless melody that guides our way.
In this orchestra of life, we shall thrive,
In the symphony of love, we are alive.

Embracing the Open Skies

With arms wide open, we'll take the leap,
Into the skies, our dreams run deep.
Beneath the sun, our spirits rise,
In the boundless realm, where hope lies.

The breeze carries whispers, soft and clear,
Promises of adventures drawing near.
In the vibrant hues of the setting sun,
Embracing the journey, our hearts as one.

Through valleys and peaks, we wander free,
The world a canvas, just you and me.
With every sunset, a chance to see,
The beauty of life, in harmony.

In the night's embrace, stars guide our way,
Illuminating paths where dreams can play.
In the vastness, we'll find our place,
Embracing the open skies with grace.

With every dawn, a fresh embrace,
A journey unfolds, time cannot erase.
So let us soar, let our spirits fly,
In the warmth of love, we touch the sky.

Flocks of Laughter

In the meadow, voices rise,
Children play beneath the skies.
Joyful echoes fill the air,
Laughter dances everywhere.

Butterflies flit, colors bright,
Chasing dreams in pure delight.
Moments shared, so light and free,
Flocks of laughter, wild and glee.

Under trees, we run and roam,
In this space, we find our home.
Warming sun, a gentle kiss,
In each heartbeat, purest bliss.

As twilight casts a golden hue,
Friendships spark, forever true.
Weaving tales of days gone past,
In our hearts, these joys will last.

With every step, our spirits soar,
In the magic, we explore.
In the shadows, still we sing,
Flocks of laughter, life’s sweet spring.

Sunlit Trails of Euphoria

Chasing rays where shadows fade,
Joyful moments, memories made.
On sunlit paths, we wander wide,
Together we embrace the tide.

Mountains call, a wild embrace,
Nature sings, an endless grace.
With every breath, we feel alive,
On these trails, our souls revive.

Golden dawns and dusky nights,
Starlit skies, the heart ignites.
In the whispers of the breeze,
Euphoria flows, a sweet tease.

Running rivers, hills so steep,
In our laughter, moments leap.
Journey endless, love’s a spark,
Through sunlit trails, we leave our mark.

As horizons stretch and bend,
In every step, the joy transcends.
Together bound, come what may,
In sunlit trails, forever stay.

Cresting on Brilliant Zephyrs

With open arms, we ride the breeze,
Cresting high on whispered trees.
The world below, a canvas bright,
We soar together, pure delight.

Each zephyr sings, a gentle tune,
Dancing beneath the silver moon.
In the hush, our spirits twine,
Brilliant whispers, yours and mine.

Fields of gold beneath our flight,
Painting dreams with purest light.
Together, hearts in wild pursuit,
Cresting on winds, we take root.

Mountains echo our joy-filled cries,
In every laugh, the world complies.
As we glide on currents fair,
Life's a journey, beyond compare.

In the twilight, shadows stretch,
In this moment, we are etched.
Cresting on brilliant zephyrs high,
Together always, you and I.

Ethereal Journeys

Through starlit realms, we glide and sway,
Ethereal dreams, we drift away.
In the stillness, peace we find,
Journeys weave, hearts intertwined.

Echoes of laughter fill the night,
Guided by the soft moonlight.
Every step, a cosmic dance,
In reverie, we take our chance.

With every wish upon a star,
Traveling near, yet far, so far.
In every moment, magic grows,
Ethereal paths, the heart knows.

Gentle breezes, whispers low,
The universe puts on a show.
As we wander, dreams will guide,
On this journey, love's our pride.

Together we explore the night,
In every shadow, sparks of light.
Ethereal journeys, ever bold,
In our souls, the stories told.

Whispers of Liberation

In shadows deep, we find our voice,
A silent cry, a fervent choice.
Chains that bind begin to break,
We rise anew, for freedom's sake.

The dawn appears, a blazing flame,
With each step forward, we reclaim.
A whispered hope, soft yet strong,
Together we stand, where we belong.

Through fields of doubt, we tread with grace,
Our spirits soar, we find our space.
With every heart, we stitch a thread,
A tapestry, where dreams are spread.

The journey’s long, but we're not alone,
In unity’s song, our hearts have grown.
We leave behind what once confined,
With weary joys, a life defined.

Each step a dance, a bold refrain,
The weight of past melts like the rain.
In whispers soft, our story told,
A tale of courage, brave and bold.

Skies Adorned with Laughter

Beneath a sky of vibrant hue,
Laughter rings, both bright and true.
Clouds like cotton, fluffy and light,
They dance and drift, a sheer delight.

Winds of joy swirl through the air,
Carrying dreams without a care.
Sunbeams trickle, warm and sweet,
As children's voices play at their feet.

A symphony of giggles rise,
Reaching up to kiss the skies.
Each note a spark, brilliantly spun,
Reminding us how life is fun.

In every heart, a playful tune,
As we sway beneath the moon.
The stars wink down, a playful spark,
Illuminating love's bright arc.

Joyous echoes fill the night,
With every breath, our spirits light.
In laughter's hoot, we find our place,
A moment held, a warm embrace.

Airborne Bliss

With arms outstretched, we touch the sky,
On wings of dreams, we dare to fly.
The world below, a distant sight,
In airborne bliss, we feel the light.

Clouds embrace us, soft and warm,
In their cocoon, we’re safe from harm.
Weightless hearts in a realm of blue,
We reach for all that's bright and true.

A gentle breeze sings in our ears,
Carrying away our doubts and fears.
We twirl and dance in open air,
In this free space, we have a care.

Through sunsets painted in glowing sheen,
We glide on dreams, so pure, serene.
In every breath, a taste of love,
As we soar high, like stars above.

And when the earth calls us back home,
With hearts ablaze, no more to roam.
We bring the sky within our soul,
In airborne bliss, we are whole.

The Elegance of a Carefree Journey

With every step, the world unfolds,
A tale of grace, as life beholds.
We wander freely, hearts aglow,
In beauty's arms, we learn to flow.

Paths unknown, yet we embrace,
The fleeting moments, time and space.
Each breath a dance, each smile a song,
In this journey, we can't go wrong.

With laughter as our guiding star,
We travel near, we travel far.
In every glance, a spark ignites,
The elegance in simple sights.

Through valleys low and mountains high,
We chase the clouds, we touch the sky.
In every twist, our spirits soar,
Embracing life forevermore.

So let us roam, through sun and shade,
In every step, the memories made.
With open hearts, a journey grand,
Together we rise, hand in hand.

Flight of the Daring Dreamers

They soar on wings of hope and light,
With hearts ablaze, they chase the night.
Above the clouds, where visions gleam,
They pierce the heavens, bold and keen.

With every gust, their spirits rise,
Unfurling dreams beneath the skies.
Adventure calls, a siren's song,
In boundless air, they all belong.

Through tempests fierce and skies so wide,
They navigate the winds with pride.
Each daring leap, a chance to fly,
On trails of stardust, they will try.

Their laughter echoes, sweet and bright,
In twilight's dance, they claim the night.
The world below begins to fade,
With every flight, their dreams cascade.

So let them soar, these dreamers bold,
In skies of azure, tales unfold.
For in their hearts, the fire beams,
In every flight, the daring dreams.

The Radiance of Laughter

In sunlit glades, where shadows play,
Laughter rings out, brightening the day.
Like blossoms swaying in the breeze,
It dances lightly among the trees.

With every chuckle, joy ignites,
Dispelling gloom, reaching new heights.
A symphony of sounds, so sweet,
Laughter's embrace, a blissful treat.

Through trials tough and paths unclear,
A joyful heart will persevere.
For in the light of playful glee,
We find our strength, we learn to be.

Each smile shared, a treasure rare,
Binding souls with love and care.
In every giggle, a song is sung,
A melody of hope, forever young.

So let us laugh, let spirits soar,
In radiant joy, we'll seek for more.
For life's embrace, so warm and bright,
Is found within the pure delight.

High Above the World Below

Upon the peaks, where eagles soar,
The quiet breathes, forevermore.
A tapestry of earth and sky,
Where dreams unfurl and whispers fly.

In crisp, clear air, the soul takes wing,
The heart ignites, as nature sings.
With every view, horizons blend,
A panoramic tale, no end.

The valleys whisper secrets old,
In shadows cast and stories told.
Each step a journey, each breath a chance,
To dance with clouds in a waltzing trance.

High above, the world feels small,
Yet in this vastness, we find it all.
With open arms, the sky we greet,
In tranquil highlands, life's bittersweet.

So let us climb where silence reigns,
To taste the peace that silence gains.
For in these heights, we're free to roam,
Finding our hearts, we find our home.

Chasing Sunbeams

With laughter bright, we chase the day,
Through fields of gold, where shadows play.
In every ray, a promise shines,
A world of wonder, where hope entwines.

We dance on paths of glowing light,
With dreams as soft as clouds in flight.
Every moment, a spark ignites,
In cherished memories, pure delights.

As twilight whispers, soft and low,
We follow sunbeams, hearts aglow.
In gentle hues of pink and red,
We weave our stories, joyfully spread.

Through meadows vast, we run and spin,
In nature's arms, all fears grow thin.
With every sunbeam that we chase,
We find our joy, our sacred place.

So let us wander, hand in hand,
With every heartbeat, ever grand.
For in the chase, our spirits soar,
In sunlit dreams, forevermore.

Soaring Spirits

Up above the world we rise,
Carried by the winds so bold,
In the light where freedom lies,
Hearts alight, stories untold.

Eagles soar with grace in flight,
Chasing dreams across the blue,
Guided by the stars at night,
Every moment feels so true.

Whispers echo in the breeze,
Nature's breath, a gentle guide,
In the rustle of the leaves,
Our spirits learn to glide.

Flowing like a river's stream,
Boundless as the open skies,
Carving paths through every dream,
With each beat, our souls arise.

Lost within the endless height,
We embrace the wild and free,
In our hearts, a pure delight,
Soaring high, eternally.

Beneath the Sky's Embrace

Underneath the vast expanse,
Lies a world both bright and wide,
In the stillness, we find chance,
To let go and just abide.

Clouds drift like thoughts on the air,
Painting dreams in softest hue,
Every moment, free from care,
Life unfolds in shades of blue.

Raindrops dance on thirsty ground,
Whispered tales of renewal,
In their rhythm, hope is found,
Embracing life's own jewel.

Stars ignite the dusky veil,
Guiding homes from distant shores,
In their glow, we set our sail,
To where longing always soars.

Hand in hand, we wander far,
Beneath the sky's gentle touch,
Finding strength in every scar,
In this vastness, we are such.

Dance of the Celestial Birds

In the twilight, colors blend,
Wings unfurl, a graceful sweep,
Dancing dreams that never end,
Through the skies, our spirits leap.

Feathers glisten in the light,
Each a note in nature's song,
Chasing shadows, pure delight,
Harmony where we belong.

In the twilight's warm embrace,
We are free to spread our wings,
Lost in joy, a boundless chase,
Life's sweet tune in whispers sings.

From the mountains to the sea,
Every place a chance to twirl,
In this dance we find the key,
To the secrets of the world.

Woven within starlit skies,
Every note a pulse of grace,
Soaring high, we realize,
Find our place in time and space.

Whispers of Freedom

Through the forest, voices call,
Echoes of a spirit free,
In the shadows of the tall,
Life unfolds a mystery.

Softly sighs the gentle breeze,
Carrying our dreams so high,
In the rustling of the leaves,
Hear the whispers as they fly.

Boundless skies and open roads,
Every step a tale to weave,
In our hearts, the silence goes,
Telling truths we dare believe.

With each dawn, a fresh new start,
Stars retreat, the sun will rise,
In the stillness, feel the heart,
Break the chains and touch the skies.

Celebrate the wild unknown,
In the journey, we belong,
Finding wings that we have sown,
Life's sweet whispers, brave and strong.

A Dance Between Clouds

The sky unfolds, a canvas bright,
Whispers of dreams take gentle flight.
Waltzing shadows, soft and free,
In the arms of eternity.

Above the world, where silence sings,
Clouds embrace on silver wings.
Eager hearts drift and sway,
In a dance where night meets day.

Sunset paints with hues so bold,
Each stroke a story waiting to be told.
With every twirl, a secret revealed,
In the heavens, our fate is sealed.

Swaying gracefully, they intertwine,
Nature's ballet, a sight divine.
Above the realm of dust and gray,
Lost in the dance, we float away.

Together they weave a tapestry,
Of joy and peace, wild and free.
As the stars awaken to shine,
In the dance of clouds, we feel divine.

The Enchantment of Flight

A bird takes wing, sharp and bright,
Soars beyond the morning light.
With every beat, the air sings free,
In the symphony of destiny.

Above the trees, the world unfolds,
Stories whispered, dreams retold.
In the winds that rush and flow,
An endless journey, far they go.

Feathers brush against the sky,
In the dance where spirits fly.
A canvas wide, so vast, so clear,
In the moment, time disappears.

Gracefully gliding, they find their way,
Through clouds and colors, night and day.
Every leap a breath of grace,
In the embrace of boundless space.

The magic sparkles, ignites the soul,
With each ascent, we feel whole.
The enchantment of flight, forever bright,
Guides us home through the starry night.

Lifted by Laughter

In shadows cast, a giggle shared,
A gentle balm, a heart repaired.
Laughter dances, pure and true,
Creating warmth in all we do.

With playful jest, the spirits soar,
Unburdened, light, we crave for more.
Echoes of joy in the air,
A reminder that love is rare.

Moments caught in time's embrace,
Fleeting yet cherished, we find our place.
In laughter's light, we rise and glide,
Together we conquer the rising tide.

A symphony of smiles, bright and grand,
With every chuckle, hand in hand.
In each heartbeat, a joyful song,
Lifted by laughter, we all belong.

So let us laugh, let worries flee,
In moments shared, together, we see.
With joy as our guide, we'll dance the night,
Lifted by laughter, hearts alight.

Luminous Voyagers

Stars in the night, a dazzling sight,
Luminous voyagers, taking flight.
Across the cosmos, wide and deep,
They weave through dreams while the world sleeps.

In their glow, stories are spun,
Galaxies twirl, and journeys begun.
With each shimmer, they share their lore,
Guiding the hearts that yearn for more.

Constellations painted in endless skies,
Whispers of wisdom, ancient and wise.
From dusk till dawn, they softly gleam,
Lighting the pathways of our dreams.

Through the veil of night, they dance and sway,
Echoing wishes that drift away.
In their embrace, we find our song,
Luminous voyagers, where we belong.

So with every twinkle, hope takes flight,
A reminder we're never alone at night.
Together we wander, under starlit skies,
In the embrace of the night, our spirits arise.

Seraphic Glides Above

Angelic whispers fill the air,
Wings that shimmer, light as prayer.
Floating softly, a dance divine,
In the skies where stars align.

Clouds embrace the gentle flight,
Carrying dreams through day and night.
Softly gliding, free and bold,
In their grace, sweet stories told.

Seraphic trails in glimmering hues,
Painting tales in varied views.
Each descent, a soft caress,
In their dance, pure tenderness.

They drift on currents, soft and bright,
Guiding hearts with pure delight.
In their wake, the world ignites,
With hopes and joys, like shooting lights.

A symphony in skies above,
Nature's blessing, purest love.
With every glide, they sing so free,
In their presence, eternity.

Choreography of the Sky

Up above, the clouds perform,
In formations, soft and warm.
Twisting, turning, a graceful show,
To the rhythm of winds that blow.

Dancing shadows, light and shade,
In the sky, a grand parade.
With each movement, tales unfold,
Whispers of ancient magic told.

The sun sets low, the colors blend,
A masterpiece that knows no end.
Cotton candy, twilight dreams,
Flowing through the golden beams.

Stars leap forth as night descends,
Joining in where daylight ends.
A cosmic ballet in the deep,
Kisses the earth as we drift to sleep.

Each ephemeral stroke they make,
Crafting beauty as they wake.
The sky, a canvas ever wide,
In synchrony, they glide and slide.

Breeze-Kissed Horizons

Horizon glows with a dawn's embrace,
A gentle breeze, a tender grace.
Whispers travel like secrets shared,
In the quiet, dreams are bared.

Fields of green greet the sun's first light,
Nature dances in pure delight.
Colors burst, a vivid spree,
Chasing shadows, wild and free.

Mountains towering, strong and grand,
Holding secrets of the land.
With each gust, a story spun,
Of how earth and sky are one.

Oceans shimmer, reflections play,
Embracing shores in soft array.
With each wave, a kiss so true,
Horizon stretches, ever new.

In this space where air meets sea,
Life unfolds in symphony.
Breeze-kissed whispers, timeless chords,
String the hearts of all aboard.

Skylight Serenade

Moonlight dances on silver seas,
Softly swaying in the breeze.
Stars adorn the velvet night,
With each glimmer, pure delight.

A serenade beneath the sky,
Nature's lullaby, a gentle sigh.
Crickets chirp in rhythmic tune,
Echoing dreams beneath the moon.

Clouds drift softly, shadows play,
Weaving magic, night and day.
With every breath, the world unwinds,
To the lull of the night it binds.

In this moment, time stands still,
Filled with wonder, hearts can fill.
As starlit breezes whisper near,
A serenade for all to hear.

So close your eyes and drift away,
In this nocturnal ballet.
Underneath the tapestry,
The sky sings sweetly, wild and free.

Soaring Revelations

In the quiet dawn, thoughts take flight,
Whispers of truth in the morning light.
Wings of insight glide through the air,
Unraveling mysteries, laying them bare.

Thoughts like feathers, soft and free,
Carried away by the gentle sea.
Each moment a spark, each glance a chance,
To dance with the clouds in a timeless romance.

From heights unseen, the ground looks small,
Perspectives shift; we rise, we fall.
In revelations bright, we find our way,
Guided by stars on the path of the day.

Awakening echoes, deep in the soul,
Fragments of stories that make us whole.
As the sun climbs high, we chase the glow,
In the realm of dreams, we learn to know.

With every breath, a story unfurls,
Painted in colors that the heart whirls.
Soaring revelations lead us to find,
The beauty in journeys, both cruel and kind.

Uplifted Spirits in the Breeze

Gentle breezes whisper through the trees,
Carrying laughter, dancing with ease.
Melodies woven in the bright air,
Uplifted spirits, free from despair.

In the meadow's glow, we twirl and spin,
With open hearts where joy begins.
Through fields of blossoms, laughter rings,
Connecting us all, the love that clings.

As the sun dips low, colors ignite,
Filling the evening with radiant light.
We gather close, dreams intertwine,
In the embrace of the night, divine.

With every gust, we rise and soar,
Breaking the chains and longing for more.
Each gentle push cradles our dreams,
As we drift along on shimmering beams.

In the breeze, our spirits unite,
Casting away shadows, embracing the light.
Together we dance on this vibrant stage,
Uplifted souls, the dawn of a new page.

Celestial Dances of Freedom

Underneath the vast, endless sky,
Stars twinkle fiercely, as dreams fly high.
In cosmic rhythms, we find our grace,
Celestial dances weave a sacred space.

The moon beckons softly, with gentle sway,
Guiding our hearts along the Milky Way.
Every step taken in shimmering hues,
Frees our spirits, with nothing to lose.

Galaxies swirl in a choreographed spin,
Inviting us inward, where journeys begin.
Floating like stardust, we twirl and dive,
In the depths of the night, we truly thrive.

With every heartbeat, the cosmos sings,
Syncing our souls to the joy that it brings.
In freedom's embrace, we chase the light,
Celestial dances, our endless flight.

So let us twine under skies so vast,
Connected by dreams, unbroken, steadfast.
In the grand tapestry of night's embrace,
We find our freedom, our sacred place.

The Magic of Elevated Dreams

Dreams arise like the morning sun,
Painted in colors, the day's begun.
With whispers of hope on the gentle breeze,
We awaken to magic with hearts at ease.

In the realm of thoughts, possibilities bloom,
Where visions blossom, dispelling the gloom.
Each aspiration a step, each wish a part,
We nurture the dreams that dwell in our heart.

Floating above in a sky of our own,
In enchanted moments, we have grown.
With courage unfurled, we chase delight,
Transforming the shadows into pure light.

The magic unfolds in the still of the night,
With stars as our guide, everything feels right.
In the tapestry woven with threads of desire,
We kindle our passion, igniting the fire.

As the world awakens, let's rise and gleam,
In the dance of existence, we live our dream.
With open hearts, let's soar ever high,
In the magic of life, together we fly.

A Carousel of Soaring Dreams

Round and round, the colors spin,
A dance of joy, a world within.
Each horse a dream, a tale to tell,
With every turn, we weave our spell.

Laughter echoes in the night,
Children's eyes, so pure, so bright.
On painted steeds, we ride so high,
Together we chase the moonlit sky.

Time stands still, we hold on tight,
To spiraled hopes and pure delight.
With every beat, our hearts align,
A carousel, where dreams entwine.

The music plays, a sweet refrain,
Carving paths in joy and pain.
Each rise and fall, a story told,
In this round world, our hearts unfold.

As dawn breaks softly on the scene,
We cherish dreams, both bright and keen.
In every spin, a spark ignites,
A carousel of soaring heights.

Cloudbound Laughs

Up above, the soft clouds float,
Laughter dances, joy’s own boat.
Tickled by winds, we share our glee,
In this sky, we roam so free.

Whispers of dreams in fluffy white,
They drift like thoughts in morning light.
Each giggle caught in sunlight's gleam,
Building castles, a child’s dream.

Fleeting moments, we chase the sun,
Cloudbound laughter has just begun.
Floating high on gentle sighs,
Where every smile and joy will rise.

Cotton candy clouds above,
Wrap us in a world of love.
As we leap, our spirits soar,
Seizing laughter, forevermore.

In this realm where shadows play,
We cherish every bright array.
Cloudbound laughs, a sacred space,
Where joy and wonder interlace.

Freedom's Elegant Leap

With open arms, we face the breeze,
Unchained minds, with hearts at ease.
A graceful dance, we rise and fall,
In freedom's embrace, we hear the call.

Through fields of gold, we run so fast,
Each moment fleeting, yet meant to last.
With every step, the world delights,
In freedom's leap, we reach new heights.

The wings of hope unfold with grace,
In every smile, a warm embrace.
We glide through dreams, like birds in flight,
In freedom's dance, we shine so bright.

Beyond the chains that once held tight,
We grasp the day, we greet the night.
A journey bold, with spirits high,
In freedom's leap, we touch the sky.

Together strong, we carve our way,
In unity, we join the play.
With open hearts, we make our mark,
In freedom's leap, we catch the spark.

Flight Path to Happiness

Wings spread wide, we take our flight,
Chasing dreams with pure delight.
Through storms and sun, we find our way,
On paths to joy, we'll dance and sway.

With every beat, our spirits soar,
Life's a journey, an open door.
Navigating through skies so blue,
In every breath, the world's anew.

Time is fleeting, but hearts hold tight,
To memories that shine so bright.
In laughter's echo, we draw near,
Finding happiness, year by year.

As stars align and dreams ignite,
We lift each other, taking flight.
With faith as our guide, we rise above,
On a flight path painted with love.

In soft landings, our souls embrace,
In every moment, a sweet grace.
Together bound, we journey far,
On this flight path, we find who we are.

Whimsical Journeys Above

In the sky where dreams take flight,
Clouds become our feathered sails,
Chasing stars through the endless night,
Whispers of wind tell playful tales.

Adventures waiting just ahead,
Painted horizons, bright and bold,
Every step a story thread,
In colors vibrant, tales unfold.

With laughter carried on the breeze,
We dance among the moonlit beams,
Each journey blessed with gentle ease,
In a landscape rich with shimmering dreams.

Through valleys lush and mountains high,
We wander free, hearts wild and light,
As silhouettes against the sky,
In this grand tapestry of night.

Together we write our own lore,
With every twist and held embrace,
Whimsical paths we can explore,
In the magic of this sacred space.

The Spirit’s Exuberant Flight

On wings of joy, we soar so high,
Dancing with clouds, we’re free as air,
In sunshine’s glow, we laugh and sigh,
Awakening dreams tossed in the flare.

With each heartbeat, a melody plays,
A symphony of unfettered light,
Through canyons deep and endless bays,
The spirit’s song ignites the night.

In fields of gold where flowers bloom,
We twirl with whispers of the breeze,
Chasing the shadows, we dispel gloom,
In nature’s arms, we find our ease.

The winds caress our wanting hearts,
Inviting hope with every lift,
As day breaks bright, and light imparts,
A breath of life, the greatest gift.

With spirits high, we ride the swell,
No bounds to hold our laughter bright,
In every moment, joy does dwell,
In the spirit's exuberant flight.

Rising with the Winds of Change

As dawn breaks forth with golden light,
We gather dreams like autumn leaves,
Casting away the shadows' fright,
Embracing change as the heart believes.

Each gust, a chance to shed the past,
With open arms, we greet the new,
In fleeting moments, memories cast,
A tapestry of vibrant hue.

Our souls awake, the world ignites,
Navigating paths we dare to take,
Through storm and calm, our spirit fights,
With every twist, we bend, not break.

Soaring high on wings of hope,
With courage penned in every line,
We find our strength, we learn to cope,
In the dance of fate, we intertwine.

With hearts aligned, we rise and sing,
Together, hand in hand, we roam,
In every heartbeat, joy we bring,
Rising with the winds of change, our home.

In the Wake of Merriment

With laughter echoing through the air,
Joy spills forth like wine so sweet,
Every heart a canvas bare,
In the wake of merriment, we meet.

Beneath the stars, we gather in cheer,
Stories shared 'neath the moon's soft glow,
Time stands still, with friends so dear,
In the rhythm of love, our spirits flow.

Playful spirits dance and sway,
In the breeze, we lift our voice,
Celebrating life in a grand ballet,
In this moment, we rejoice.

With colors bright, our laughter blooms,
Painting the night with dreams unspun,
Magic lingers in brightly lit rooms,
Every heartbeat a race we've won.

In joy's embrace, we find our place,
Creating memories that intertwine,
In the wake of merriment's grace,
Life's sweetest moments become divine.

Fantasies on the Wind

Whispers dance through open skies,
Secrets carried on the breeze.
Clouds are dreams with hidden sighs,
Softly rustling through the trees.

A fluttering heart takes its flight,
Where wishes mingle with the stars.
In the hush of velvet night,
We find our peace, we heal our scars.

Tales of wonder sweep the land,
In every gust, a story glows.
With every breath, new worlds expand,
And in their arms, our spirit flows.

Chasing echoes of the past,
We weave our dreams upon the gale.
In laughter, memories are cast,
As dreams unfurl like ships with sail.

Fantasies on the wind shall soar,
Boundless realms await the bold.
From every heart, love's whisper roars,
In every turn, new tales unfold.

Luminous Feathers of Delight

In the morning's gentle light,
Colors burst like whispers sweet.
Feathers glimmer, pure and bright,
Nature’s canvas, bold and fleet.

Dance of joy in every hue,
Sparkling in the dawn's embrace.
Luminous dreams that feel so new,
Catch the sunlight with their grace.

Wings of laughter take to air,
Floating freely, wild and bold.
Life's sweet magic everywhere,
Stories in each feather told.

Softly tracing paths of glee,
Through the gardens, boundless, wide.
In this realm, the heart is free,
Where all sorrows turn to pride.

Luminous feathers drift and sway,
Carrying whispers of our dreams.
In their beauty, hope will stay,
Reflecting joy in sunlit streams.

Revelry on High

On the mountaintop we dance,
Hearts alight with fervent cheer.
In the stars, we find our chance,
To lift our voices, bold and clear.

Moonlit pathways call us near,
Underneath the heavens' art.
In the stillness, we adhere,
To the rhythms of the heart.

Echoes of our laughter blend,
With the notes of night's sweet song.
In this moment, joy won't end,
For together, we belong.

Hands entwined, we brave the heights,
Every twirl a spark of grace.
Through the whirlwind of the nights,
We find our true and cherished place.

Revelry in every breath,
A celebration of our light.
In this joy, we conquer death,
As we dance in pure delight.

Where Lightness Takes Flight

In a realm where spirits soar,
Every heartbeat sings with bliss.
Weightless dreams on breezes pour,
Kissed by sunshine's tender kiss.

Floating high above the ground,
Joy cascades in streams of gold.
Lightness in the air is found,
In the stories yet untold.

Wings of laughter, soft and true,
Carry whispers of the day.
Guiding hearts to skies so blue,
Where the shadows fade away.

In this haven, joy ignites,
As we twirl through open skies.
Here in peace, our spirit writes,
Songs of love that never die.

Where lightness takes us by the hand,
We embrace the endless flight.
In the beauty of this land,
We'll weave our dreams into the night.

Pilgrims of the Air

With wings of dreams, we ascend high,
Through clouds of hope, where spirits fly.
Each gust a whisper, a guiding hand,
Together we journey, a faithful band.

The sun paints gold on our eager backs,
As we navigate the silver tracks.
The world below, a distant song,
In the sky's embrace, we all belong.

With every heartbeat, the universe calls,
In this vast expanse, we break down walls.
The horizon beckons, a canvas bright,
Pilgrims of air, we chase the light.

Through storms and shadows, we hold on tight,
In the dance of freedom, we find our flight.
The journey is long, but our spirits soar,
In the arms of the sky, we seek for more.

Together we soar, no limits to bind,
In the heart of the winds, our fate aligned.
On currents of dreams, we rise and glide,
Pilgrims of the air, forever untried.

The Dawn’s Unfurling Wings

As dawn breaks softly, the dark takes flight,
With hues of amber, the world ignites.
The sky unwinds, a tapestry spun,
In the cradle of morning, new days begun.

Birds awaken, their songs take wing,
In the heart of silence, sweet praises ring.
The light cascades, a gentle embrace,
In the dawn’s unfurling, we find our place.

With every ray, the shadows retreat,
Illuminating paths where dreamers meet.
As whispers of daybreak swirl and weave,
In the warmth of the sun, we learn to believe.

The promise of morning, a potion so dear,
In its brilliance, we cast off our fear.
The horizon stretches, a canvas anew,
The dawn’s unfurling wings bid us to pursue.

As moments unfold, we seize the day,
In the quiet of morning, dreams find their way.
With hearts open wide, we embrace the flight,
In the dawn’s embrace, all is made right.

Ascent into the Limitless

We rise on the breeze, our spirits unchained,
In a realm of wonders, where dreams are gained.
With hearts ignited, we seek the unknown,
On paths untraveled, our courage has grown.

The sky calls to us, a canvas so vast,
In the dance of the clouds, our shadows are cast.
With every heartbeat, we venture and roam,
In the cradle of air, we find our home.

Beyond the horizon, where visions reside,
An ascent into limitless, our souls glide.
With wings of ambition, we shatter the night,
In the light of the stars, we reclaim our might.

Through valleys of doubt, we soar above,
Embracing the journey, held close by love.
Like whispers of twilight, we rise and ignite,
Ascent into the limitless, our spirits take flight.

In fields of the infinite, we find our grace,
In the embrace of the sky, we find our place.
With each step we take, we honor the path,
Ascent into the limitless, igniting our wrath.

The Symphony of Gliding Hearts

In the hush of the evening, the air hums low,
A melody woven, where wild winds blow.
Hearts in unison, we rise and blend,
In the symphony of gliding, our spirits transcend.

Each note a shadow, each breath a spark,
In the dusk's embrace, we venture the dark.
With wings intertwined, we dance through the night,
Creating a cadence, a beautiful flight.

The stars our witness, the moon our guide,
In the symphony of gliding, we take pride.
With laughter like music, we follow our dreams,
Through the twilight whispers, where magic redeems.

As seasons may change, our song remains true,
In harmony's arms, we'll always renew.
In the sea of the night, we find clarity,
The symphony of gliding hearts sets us free.

With each fleeting moment, the echoes will stay,
In the dance of the stars, we'll forever play.
For together we write a timeless refrain,
The symphony of gliding hearts in the rain.

www.ingramcontent.com/pod-product-compliance
Ingram Content Group UK Ltd.
Pitfield, Milton Keynes, MK11 3LW, UK
UKHW030903221224
452712UK00007B/959